ASTRONOMY

by

TERRY MAHONEY

D0808511

1 9 MAR 2016

30130 118324945

THE STUDY OF THE PLANETS

Planetary science is the branch of astronomy that studies the planets and minor bodies of our Solar System. It brings together elements of chemistry, physics, geology and meteorology. For the last 40 years, manned and unmanned spacecraft have been sent into space. Astronauts have set foot on the Moon, while observational missions like Spacelab (*above*), have been launched high into Earth's orbit. Unmanned space satellites and probes continue to revolutionize planetary science. They have visited remote worlds in our Solar System, sending back a wealth of information to eager astronomers on Earth.

WHAT IS ASTRONOMY?

How big is the Universe? **What is it made of? How old is it? Is there life on other planets?** Man has always been fascinated by the night sky, puzzling at exactly what makes up the vast expanses of space. Astronomy is the observational science that attempts to answer these questions. It consists of many different scientific disciplines, such as planetary science, cosmology, astrobiology and astrophysics.

POSITIONAL ASTRONOMY

The very first thing we need to know about an astronomical object is where to find it and how it moves in space. Before the invention of the telescope, astronomers used tools such as this armillary sphere to navigate their way around the night sky. Nowadays, astronomers use telescopes and satellites to pinpoint accurately the positions of stars and planets in the sky and to track their movements in space and time.

THE BIG QUESTIONS

Cosmology is the branch of astronomy that looks at the Universe as a whole. It became a proper science during the first half of the 20th century with the building of the first generation of giant telescopes and the general theory of relativity, devised by Albert Einstein (1879–1955). His theory explains how galaxies, black holes and even the Universe warp the space surrounding them (as shown in the centre of the above image). Today, cosmologists wrestle with questions such as exactly how the Universe came into being and how it might eventually come to an end.

ARE WE ALONE?

Many of us believe that there probably is life elsewhere in the Universe. Since the 1950s, radio, television and magazines (such as this one) have fuelled our suspicions by imaginatively depicting alien life forms. Exobiology (or astrobiology) is the branch of astronomy that examines the chances of finding life on other planets. The possibilities of finding some form of life on Mars have not yet been discounted, while another possible haven for life is Europa, a moon of Jupiter which might have oceans able to support life beneath its icy crust.

STARGAZING

Astrophysics began in the 1860s, following the identification of several chemical elements in the Sun and other stars. The name means simply 'the physics of the stars'. This type of astronomy analyses starlight, which can help explain the structure and evolution of galaxies. Astrophysicists have discovered, for example, that the long, dark dust lanes of the magnificent Whirlpool galaxy (*above*) are actually nurseries for future generations of stars.

TRICKS & TECHNIQUES

In 1609, the Italian astronomer Galileo revolutionized astronomy when he used a home-made telescope to view the heavens. Today, astronomers can launch probes into the depths of the Solar System to send back new information, while space telescopes feed back huge amounts of data on the stars and galaxies. Although there are many kinds of telescope, they are all built to do two things — to collect as much light as possible and to provide the most detailed images. Both of these properties depend on the size of the collecting lens or mirror.

SPACE PROBES

Unfortunately it will not be possible for humans to visit many parts of the Solar System because of the extreme dangers involved. However, it has been possible for astronomers to send robotic probes to planets in the Solar System and beyond. These probes relay images to Earth via radio signals from TV cameras, while other onboard instruments take a range of measurements.

RADIO TELESCOPES

Radio telescopes were first used in the 1940s to detect radio signals from space. Many objects in the Universe, from stars to galaxies, emit radio waves. Because radio waves are longer than light waves, radio telescopes need to be bigger than ordinary telescopes to capture the same amount of detail. Radio waves can penetrate through dust clouds that block visible light, and have been used to map the Milky Way (*see pages 22-23*).

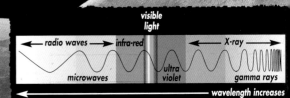

radio waves → infra-red → visible light ← X-ray →
microwaves / ultra violet / gamma rays
wavelength increases

SCIENCE EXPLAINED: THE ELECTROMAGNETIC SPECTRUM

Light is a form of radiation that is transported in waves. Each of the colours of the rainbow has its own wavelength. The entire range of wavelengths is called the electromagnetic spectrum. Unfortunately, the protective atmosphere of the Earth cuts out many of the wavelengths, but from space, the entire spectrum is visible. By studying what kind of radiation is emitted from objects such as stars, astronomers can learn about an object's density, temperature, chemical composition and how it moves.

HUBBLE SPACE TELESCOPE

Space telescopes have revolutionized astronomy. The protective atmosphere of the Earth is a menace to astronomers, because it causes the image we see through a telescope to quiver and ripple like the surface of a pond. It is this that makes the stars twinkle. In space, however, there is no atmosphere. Launched in 1990, the Hubble Space Telescope orbits about 600 km (370 miles) above the Earth, sending back startlingly clear images to astronomers.

REFLECTING TELESCOPES

Today, most telescopes built for research use mirrors to collect the light. Mirrors have several advantages over lenses. Whereas lenses create false colours, absorb light and can sag under their own weight, mirrors do not have such handicaps.

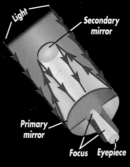

Light

Secondary mirror

Primary mirror

Focus   *Eyepiece*

1. Light falls through the top of the open-frame tube, and heads towards the primary mirror.

2. It is then reflected up the tube to the smaller, secondary mirror.

3. The light is then reflected back down the tube, through a hole in the primary, to the focus (located beneath the primary).

REFRACTING TELESCOPES

Refracting telescopes consist of two lenses — one at the front (the objective lens) and one at the back (the eyepiece, which magnifies the focused image). Today, these are less popular with professional astronomers than reflecting telescopes. Binoculars, which are popular with amateur astronomers, are twin refracting telescopes arranged side by side.

Objective lens

Focus

Eyepiece

1. The objective lens catches the light and brings it to a focus.

2. The eyepiece magnifies the focused image.

WINTER SKY

Orion, the Hunter (marked below in red), is a magnificent constellation visible during late evenings in winter.
The three stars in its belt can be used as a celestial signpost. Just below the belt is a shiny patch called the Orion Nebula, which is a splendid sight through binoculars or a small telescope. The Orion Nebula is in fact a stellar nursery, where stars are being born right now.

GEMINI
A slightly curving line drawn upwards through Rigel and Betelgeuse will get you to Gemini, with its two bright stars Castor and Pollus, the Heavenly Twins.

AURIGA
Over Orion's head is Auriga, the Charioteer. Near the bright star Capella is a distinctive triangle of stars called the Kids.

PERSEUS
Now follow a line northeast of Orion past Taurus and you will come to Perseus. This constellation contains a double open cluster (see pages 8-9), which is a great sight through binoculars.

CANIS MINOR
A line to the west of Orion takes you to the small constellation Canis Minor, the Little Dog. The three stars Procyon (in Canis Minor), Betelgeuse (in Orion) and Sirius (in Canis Major) form the prominent Winter Triangle.

TAURUS
Follow the three stars of Orion's belt upwards and you will come to the constellation Taurus, the Bull. Taurus contains the bright red star Aldebaran. This star appears to form part of the 'v' of the Hyades, which is an open star cluster. In fact, Aldebaran is a foreground star and is not part of this distant group. Following the line from Orion's belt yet further, you will come to a close-knit bunch of stars called the Pleiades. These stars form yet another open cluster.

CANIS MAJOR
Canis Major, the Big Dog, is found by following Orion's belt downwards. It contains Sirius, the brightest star in the sky.

LEPUS
Beneath Orion is an undistinguished constellation called Lepus, the Hare.

ERIDANUS
Eridanus, the River, is another faint constellation which manages to meander a sixth of the way around the sky. It lies to the right of Orion, just past Rigel.

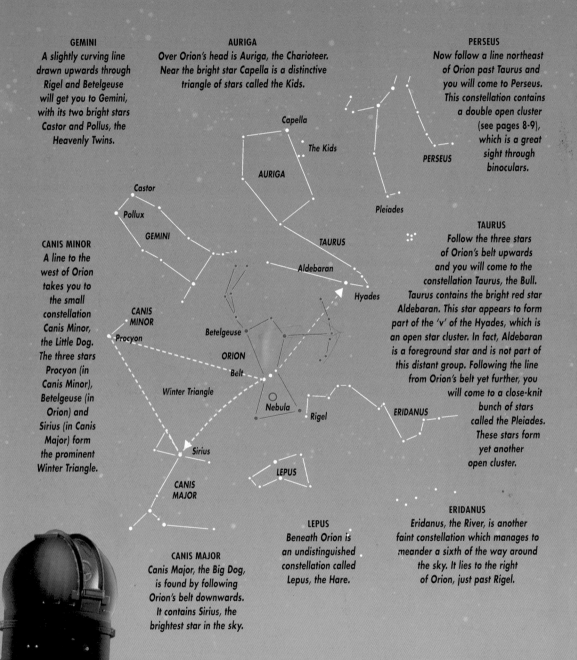

Capella · The Kids · AURIGA · PERSEUS · Pleiades · Castor · Pollux · GEMINI · TAURUS · Aldebaran · Hyades · CANIS MINOR · Betelgeuse · ORION · Procyon · Belt · Winter Triangle · Nebula · Rigel · ERIDANUS · Sirius · LEPUS · CANIS MAJOR

NAVIGATING THE NIGHT SKY

On a clear, moonless night, over 2,000 stars can be seen with the naked eye. Ancient astronomers identified star patterns, called constellations. These patterns are purely a human invention and serve only to help astronomers find their way in the sky. In reality, what looks to us like a bright star might really only be a faint star fairly close by, whereas a genuinely bright star might appear dim to us because of its vast distance from Earth.

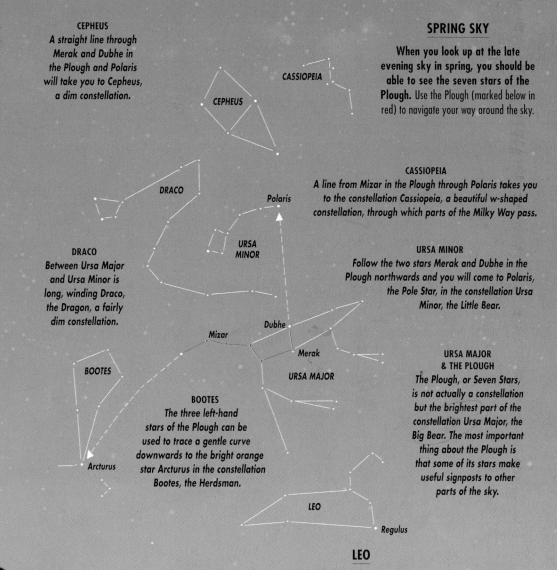

CEPHEUS
A straight line through Merak and Dubhe in the Plough and Polaris will take you to Cepheus, a dim constellation.

SPRING SKY

When you look up at the late evening sky in spring, you should be able to see the seven stars of the **Plough.** Use the Plough (marked below in red) to navigate your way around the sky.

CASSIOPEIA
A line from Mizar in the Plough through Polaris takes you to the constellation Cassiopeia, a beautiful w-shaped constellation, through which parts of the Milky Way pass.

DRACO
Between Ursa Major and Ursa Minor is long, winding Draco, the Dragon, a fairly dim constellation.

URSA MINOR
Follow the two stars Merak and Dubhe in the Plough northwards and you will come to Polaris, the Pole Star, in the constellation Ursa Minor, the Little Bear.

BOOTES
The three left-hand stars of the Plough can be used to trace a gentle curve downwards to the bright orange star Arcturus in the constellation Bootes, the Herdsman.

URSA MAJOR & THE PLOUGH
The Plough, or Seven Stars, is not actually a constellation but the brightest part of the constellation Ursa Major, the Big Bear. The most important thing about the Plough is that some of its stars make useful signposts to other parts of the sky.

LEO

Directly underneath the Plough is the constellation Leo, the Lion. It is one of the few constellations that bears even the slightest resemblance to its name. Its bright star, Regulus, is the dot in an inverted question mark of stars known as the Sickle.

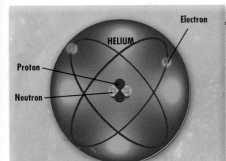

ATOMS & MOLECULES

All known matter is made of atoms, which are rather like tiny solar systems. Atoms have a central nucleus, and electrons that go round the nucleus like planets orbiting the Sun. The nucleus is usually made of two kinds of particles: protons and neutrons. Normally, there are as many orbiting electrons as there are protons in the nucleus, but sometimes an atom loses one or more of its electrons. It is then said to be ionized. The two most important atoms in astronomy are helium (*above*) and hydrogen (*below*). Helium has two orbiting electrons and a nucleus of two protons and two neutrons, while hydrogen has a single proton in its nucleus and a single orbiting electron. In space, hydrogen atoms exist either as individual atoms or stick together as molecules, while helium remains a free-floating atom. A gas of ionized atoms is called a plasma, and most of the visible matter in the Universe exists in plasma form. Plasmas are said to form the fourth state of matter (the other three forms being solid, liquid and gas).

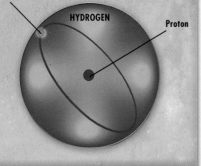

BUILDING BLOCKS OF THE UNIVERSE

Astronomy poses many big questions, such as what is the Universe made of, how did it all begin and why do stars shine. However, to understand these big concepts, it is necessary to break things down to the basics. It is by studying the smallest units that make up matter — atoms and elements — that astronomers can begin to piece together the Universe. Everything is made up of the same basic elements, and many of the reactions that take place at a small level are the same reactions that cause big events in the Universe. For example, the nuclear reactions that cause a hydrogen bomb to explode are the same reactions that cause the stars to shine.

FROM SMALL BEGINNINGS

Atoms are the smallest independent units that make up the chemistry of the Universe. Some combine in clumps called molecules. Both atoms and molecules float freely in the space between the stars. There are also dust grains, which are puffed off by giant stars. These tiny dust grains, measuring a thousandth of a millimetre across, form truly enormous clouds such as the Horsehead Nebula (*above*). These clouds are actually star factories. Eventually, the gas and dust within collapse to create new stars.

SCIENCE EXPLAINED: LIGHT YEARS

Since distances are so vast in astronomy, it makes little sense to use units such as the kilometre beyond the Solar System. Astronomers use a unit of measurement called a light year instead. Light travels 300,000 km (186,000 miles) per second. In other words, it could whip round the Earth seven times in a single second. In a year, light travels just over 9 million, million kilometres, so a light year is 9 million, million kilometres.

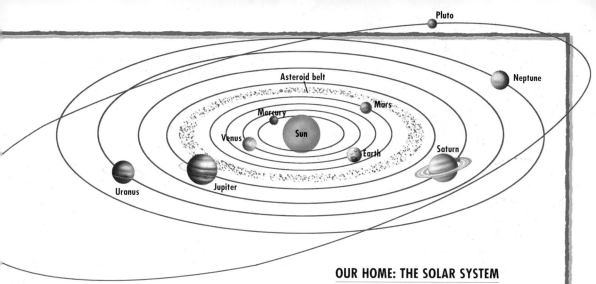

OUR HOME: THE SOLAR SYSTEM

**Our Solar System is made up of a central star (the Sun),
nine known major planets, innumerable asteroids and icy rocks (comets) that throw out tails of gas and
dust when they fall towards the Sun.** All the stars you see in the night sky lie beyond our Solar System, which is just a
tiny part of our galaxy, the Milky Way, one of countless other galaxies.

STAR GROUPINGS

Stars contain most of the visible matter in the Universe. These giant balls of hot gas do not float about individually,
but are grouped together in a number of different ways, described below.

OPEN CLUSTERS
*Stars spend their infancy in stellar nurseries, called open clusters, with up to 10,000 other stars.
Open clusters are gradually pulled apart by the gravity of their surroundings until all the stars
float freely in space. The nearest star to the Sun is just over four light years away.*

GLOBULAR CLUSTERS
*Globular clusters can contain up to a million
old stars and can be ten times the size of
open clusters. The stars in globular clusters
are tightly bound by gravity. About 140
globular clusters (like the NGC 1850 shown
right) surround our Galaxy.*

GALAXIES
*Galaxies (above)
are the biggest single
units in the Universe.
Our own Galaxy,
which measures
100,000 light years
across and contains
more than 100 billion
stars, is a fairly
average example.*

GALAXY CLUSTERS
*Galaxies do not float freely in space
but form clusters of galaxies. The Milky
Way is part of a group of 31 known
galaxies called the Local Group, which
measures about 6 million light years across.
Clusters of galaxies (left) can form larger
clusters called superclusters, measuring up
to 300 million light years across.*

THE BIRTH OF A STAR

All stars are born from clouds of dust, and end their lives in violent circumstances. They begin life as dwarfs before changing into giants or supergiants as they heat up. Depending on how much mass they start out with, they end their lives in a variety of different ways.

1. New stars all come from giant clouds of dust and gas.

2. Knots begin to form in the gas cloud as gravity pulls it together. This compression causes the cloud to heat up.

3. Eventually the gas begins to spiral round. Jets of gas are expelled from the poles.

4. The star's brightness increases as nuclear fusion begins at its centre. All the gas and dust in the space surrounding the star is blown away, and eventually the star emerges from its dusty cocoon.

5. The process is complete. The new dwarf star begins to shine, and joins the main sequence. This is the most stable period of a star's life.

SCIENCE EXPLAINED: MAKING THE PLANETS

We have a good idea about how our Sun was born, but what about the planets? As a star is formed, a disc of material surrounds it. Some is pulled back into the star by gravity. When the temperature eventually cools down, the dust that remains begins to collect together in small clumps called planetesimals. In our Solar System, some planetesimals combined to form planets. In the outer reaches, large planet cores formed that held on to some of the gas contained in the original cloud. These planets were the gas giants Jupiter, Saturn, Uranus and Neptune.

THE DEATH OF A STAR

Whether a dwarf has changed into a giant or a supergiant dictates how the star will die...

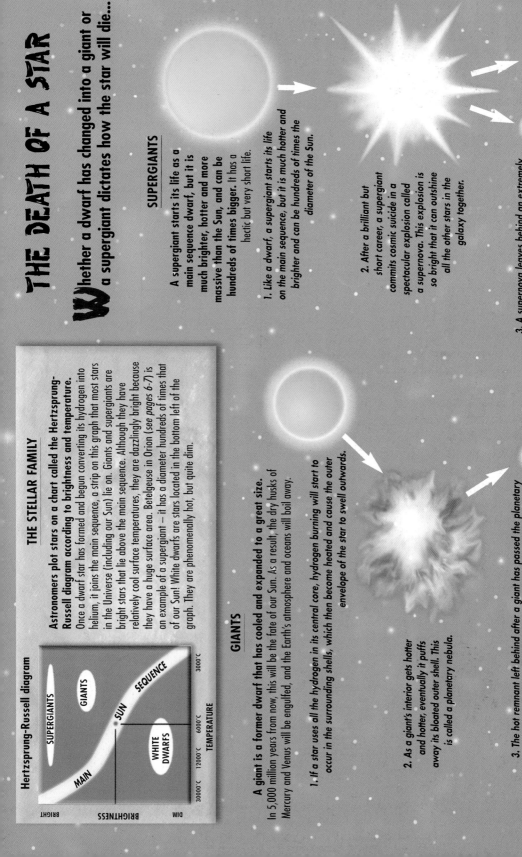

THE STELLAR FAMILY

Astronomers plot stars on a chart called the Hertzsprung-Russell diagram according to brightness and temperature. Once a dwarf star has formed and begun converting its hydrogen into helium, it joins the main sequence, a strip on this graph that most stars in the Universe (including our Sun) lie on. Giants and supergiants are bright stars that lie above the main sequence. Although they have relatively cool surface temperatures, they are dazzlingly bright because they have a huge surface area. Betelgeuse in Orion (*see pages 6-7*) is an example of a supergiant – it has a diameter hundreds of times that of our Sun! White dwarfs are stars located in the bottom left of the graph. They are phenomenally hot, but quite dim.

Hertzsprung-Russell diagram

(chart showing:)
SUPERGIANTS
GIANTS
SUN
MAIN SEQUENCE
WHITE DWARFS

BRIGHT — BRIGHTNESS — DIM

TEMPERATURE
30000°C 12000°C 6000°C 3000°C

SUPERGIANTS

A supergiant starts its life as a main sequence dwarf, but it is much brighter, hotter and more massive than the Sun, and can be hundreds of times bigger. It has a hectic but very short life.

1. Like a dwarf, a supergiant starts its life on the main sequence, but it is much hotter and brighter and can be hundreds of times the diameter of the Sun.

2. After a brilliant but short career, a supergiant commits cosmic suicide in a spectacular explosion called a supernova. This explosion is so bright that it can outshine all the other stars in the galaxy together.

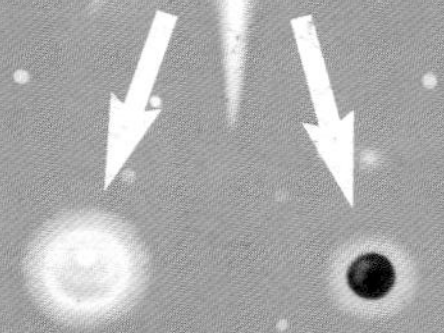

3. A supernova leaves behind an extremely dense remnant such as a neutron star or a black hole (see pages 24-25).

GIANTS

A giant is a former dwarf that has cooled and expanded to a great size. In 5,000 million years from now, this will be the fate of our Sun. As a result, the dry husks of Mercury and Venus will be engulfed, and the Earth's atmosphere and oceans will boil away.

1. If a star uses all the hydrogen in its central core, hydrogen burning will start to occur in the surrounding shells, which then become heated and cause the outer envelope of the star to swell outwards.

2. As a giant's interior gets hotter and hotter, eventually it puffs away its bloated outer shell. This is called a planetary nebula.

3. The hot remnant left behind after a giant has passed the planetary nebula stage is called a white dwarf. The gravity of white dwarfs is so intense that the result is an Earth-sized remnant so dense that a matchboxful would weigh several tonnes.

Solar wind   Magnetic field

A GIANT MAGNET

The Earth is unusual in having a fairly strong magnetic field, which acts like a bar magnet at its centre. This magnetic field serves as a shield against charged particles from the Sun (the solar wind). Such particles are deadly to life, so we owe our continued existence to the Earth's magnetic field. However, when there are particularly violent storms on the Sun, the charged particles become a hazard to astronauts and manage to penetrate the upper atmosphere, causing radio interference, power cuts and the beautiful displays of the Northern Lights.

HIDE & SEEK

The Moon orbits the Earth at an average distance of 384,400 km (240,000 miles). For half of its orbit it is closer to the Sun than the Earth, and for the other half it is farther away. This means that it shows different portions of its illuminated surface to the Earth at different times, giving us what are known as the lunar phases. However, the Moon completes one spin on its axis in the same time that it takes to orbit the Earth, so it always shows the same face to the Earth. This picture, taken by the Apollo 17 astronauts, shows the borderline separating day and night on the moon.

THE WORLD OF THE MOON

The Moon's surface is divided into bright highlands and dark volcanic lava plains. The entire surface is peppered with craters caused by meteorite impacts. The Moon is an airless world and there is no liquid water on its surface. This means that the surface is exactly as it was millions of years ago. The Apollo astronauts left seismometers to measure tremors on the lunar surface. These have recorded 'moonquakes' 800 km (500 miles) underground.

EARTH & MOON — A DOUBLE ACT

Many of the planets in the Solar System have moons, and our own planet is no exception. What is special about our Moon is its size in relation to the Earth — all the other moons in the Solar System are much smaller than their central planets. The Earth has a special relationship with the Moon, which affects aspects of life on our planet. The Moon's gravitational pull (the invisible force keeping the two bodies together) is mainly responsible for tides, and is also slowly affecting the length of our days.

THE THIRD PLANET

The Earth is the third planet from the Sun, which it orbits once a year at a mean distance of 150 million km (93 million miles). It is over five times denser than water. The Earth's pole-to-pole diameter is less than its diameter measured at the Equator. This slight squashing at the poles is due to the daily rotation, which causes the Earth to bulge outwards at the Equator. This breathtaking view was taken by the crew of the Apollo 17 space mission.

A HAVEN FOR LIFE

Look at the picture above and what can you see? Clouds? Oceans? Plants? Look again and you see the vital ingredients for life — water and carbon dioxide. These features have given Earth unique conditions that have allowed life to flourish. In the search for life elsewhere in the Universe, astronomers look for water and carbon-based elements in the hope of pinpointing planets where life could, theoretically, thrive. The Earth is also invaluable for astronomers hoping to understand the make-up of similar planets in our Solar System. Geologists know the deep internal structure of the Earth from measuring seismic waves from earthquakes, and astronomers can use this information to develop a better understanding of the other Earthlike planets.

SCIENCE EXPLAINED: TIDES & GRAVITY

The level of Earth's oceans rises and falls twice a day to give us the familiar tides. Tides are caused by the combined gravitational pull of the Moon and Sun. The Moon's pull is considerably stronger, so the oceans swell into the shape of a rugby ball, with a build up of water on the side facing the Moon and another facing in the opposite direction. As the Earth rotates on its axis, different parts of the oceans are raised. The water does not move forward or back, as you might think, but actually rises and falls twice a day. Tides are not the only way in which the Moon affects our planet. The pull of its gravity is slowing down the Earth's rotation, gradually making our days longer. It is also slowly pushing the Moon further away from the Earth.

EARTHLIKE PLANETS

The four closest planets to the Sun – Mercury, Venus, Earth and Mars – form a family of small, dense rocky worlds known as the terrestrial planets because of their similarity to Earth. Although the planets can be studied with a telescope, it was not until the 1950s and the arrival of the Space Age that astronomers were able to piece together the complicated past history of our Solar System. Each planet has turned out to be unique and has provided astronomers with many surprises.

GREAT BALL OF FIRE

Venus is a forbidding and hostile world. It orbits the Sun once every 224.7 Earth days at a distance of 108 million km (67 million miles). Until Russian and American space probes reached it, little was known about this fiery world since its entire surface is permanently covered by thick clouds. A dense atmosphere of carbon dioxide traps the heat from the Sun, producing temperatures high enough to melt lead. Orbital radar probes were used by astronomers to produce a complete map of the surface of Venus, with its craters, volcanoes and mountains.

MR SPOCK & THE PLANET VULCAN

The orbit of Mercury does not quite obey Newton's theory of gravity. In 1860, the French astronomer Urbain de Leverrier made calculations suggesting the presence of an undiscovered planet inside the orbit of Mercury that was pulling Mercury off course. He named the supposed new planet Vulcan. Another astronomer also claimed to have seen such a planet passing in front of the Sun. Sadly for Mr Spock, however, Vulcan has never been seen since, and the peculiarities of Mercury's orbit can be explained by the fact that the Sun is warping the space around the planet, in accordance with Einstein's theory of relativity *(see page 2)*. Nevertheless, the search is on for a group of supposed asteroids, named vulcanoids, inside the orbit of Mercury.

THE RED PLANET

Brooding Mars has captured the imagination of artists, scholars and astronomers for hundreds of years. At 228 million km (142 million miles) from the Sun, it takes Mars 687 Earth days to complete its orbit. It has an extremely thin atmosphere and in the Martian summer dust storms cover the entire surface of the planet. The polar icecaps melt and re-form in the winter. The surface has a great variety of features, including dust dunes, craters and the mighty Olympus Mons, an extinct volcano that measures 80 km (50 miles) across and a staggering 25 km (15.5 miles) high. There is some evidence that at some time in the past, water once flowed on Mars. The image below of the surface of Mars was taken by the Viking probe, which landed on the planet in 1973, taking a series of stunning photographs.

THE ASTEROID BELT

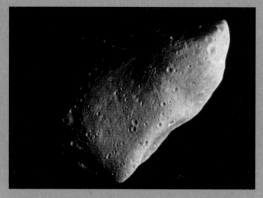

A swarm of rocky worldlets with diameters from 1–1,000 km (0.6–620 miles) orbit the Sun at distances ranging from 300–495 million km (86–307 million miles). These asteroids are very small by planetary standards and are irregular in shape. The Galileo probe produced this picture of the pitted, potato-shaped asteroid Gaspra from a distance of 1,600 km (1,000 miles). Even such small bodies as asteroids bear the scars of heavy meteorite impacts from the distant past.

SOME LIKE IT HOT

Mercury is the closest planet to the Sun, which it orbits once every 88 days at a distance of nearly 60 million km (37 million miles). Its day is 59 Earth days long. This was discovered using radar observations. In 1974, the Mariner 10 spacecraft made this montage of its surface, revealing a landscape more heavily cratered than the Moon's. The surface temperature is over 400 degrees during the Mercurian day, plummeting to almost 200 degrees below zero at night. Mercury has no atmosphere, as the intense heat of the Sun has boiled it away.

SCIENCE EXPLAINED: INTERPLANETARY TRAFFIC LAWS

The 17th-century German astronomer Johannes Kepler discovered three laws to explain how planets orbit:
1. *A planet orbits the Sun in an elliptical orbit.*
2. *Planets speed up as they get closer to the Sun, and slow down as they get farther away.*
3. *The distance of a planet from the Sun can be worked out once we know the length of its year, and the length of year and distance from the Sun of one other planet (usually the Earth).*

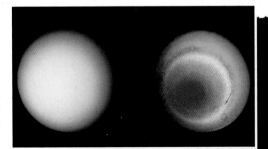

Great Dark Spot

NEPTUNE

The second farthest planet from the Sun, Neptune takes 165 Earth years to complete an orbit around the Sun. It was discovered in 1846 after its position had been predicted by John Couch Adams in England and Urbain de Leverrier in France. Adams and de Leverrier calculated Neptune's position by the pull it exerted on the neighbouring planet Uranus. Neptune is similar in structure to Uranus and has a prominent storm zone called the Great Dark Spot.

URANUS

In the right conditions, Uranus is just visible to the naked eye, but it was not until 1781 that it was discovered by Sir William Herschel. It orbits the Sun once every 84 Earth years and has the distinction of spinning almost on its side. Its seasons are peculiar, with summer and winter each lasting 20 years. The planet's rocky core is surrounded by a thick shell of ice and the atmosphere is similar to that of Jupiter.

SCIENCE EXPLAINED: MASSES & DENSITIES

Astronomers are very interested in discovering the density of a planet. A simple sum allows them to work it out – the amount of mass divided by the space (volume) the planet occupies. Astronomers know the masses and the sizes of the planets from telescopic observations and data sent back by space probes, so they can work out the densities. The Earth is about five times denser than water, typical of the terrestrial planets. Jupiter, Uranus and Neptune are slightly denser than water, while Saturn is actually less dense than water.

TOMBAUGH'S FIND

Pluto is the farthest known planet from the Sun, and was discovered in 1930 by Clyde Tombaugh (*left*). Its position had been correctly predicted earlier by Percival Lowell, but Tombaugh's planet was smaller and closer to the Sun than Lowell had predicted. Pluto is an icy world that is smaller than our Moon, and yet it has its own satellite, Charon, discovered by James Walter Christy in 1978.

GIANTS OF GAS & ICE

Beyond Mars and the asteroid belt lie four giant worlds that dwarf the Earth and its close **neighbours.** These are the mighty planets Jupiter, Saturn, Uranus and Neptune. These giants all have rings and numerous moons, and – with the exception of Uranus – they all give out more heat than they receive from the Sun. Out beyond the orbit of Neptune is the small double-world of Pluto-Charon. Astronomers are now debating whether Pluto should really be considered as a planet.

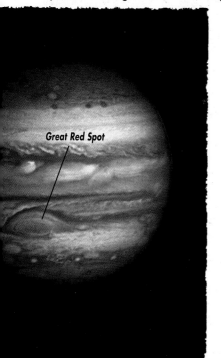

Great Red Spot

THE MOONS OF THE GIANTS

All four giant planets have large families of moons, some bigger than Mercury. Information from space probes has revealed a surprising diversity among these minor worlds. Jupiter's moon Io (*above*) is the most volcanically active world in the Solar System. The lava spouting from Io's volcanoes lands on the surface as solid lumps at the same speed as bullets from a machine gun. After Venus, Io is the most volatile world in the Solar System.

THE KING OF PLANETS

Jupiter takes 12 Earth years to complete its orbit. It is the largest of the planets and it is big enough to swallow a thousand Earths. In fact, this colossus has over twice the mass of all the other planets put together. Its rocky core is surrounded by a shell of liquid hydrogen and there is no solid surface. The thick, deep atmosphere contains mainly hydrogen and helium. The famous Great Red Spot is actually a violent storm that has been raging for centuries. The image on the left shows the planet with three of its moons – Io, Europa and Ganymede.

THE RINGED PLANET

The second largest of the planets, Saturn takes just over 29 Earth years to complete an orbit. Being less dense than water, it would float if enough water could be found to run a bath for this giant! The most striking feature of Saturn is its beautiful ring system. The rings are actually made of millions of small chunks of rock and ice. Voyager probes revealed that there are actually hundreds of individual ringlets which are divided into six groups, as shown in the false-colour image on the right.

F RING – the outermost ring

A RING – the outermost ring visible from Earth

CASSINI DIVISION – although it appears to be a gap, this region contains over 100 faint rings

B RING – the brightest and densest of the rings

C RING – this blue ring is the faintest visible from Earth

D RING – this faint ring almost touches Saturn

SOLAR SYSTEM SMALL FRY

HALLEY'S COMET

Halley's comet is probably the most famous comet of all. The Bayeux Tapestry, an embroidered artwork commissioned by William the Conqueror of England between 1067–77, depicts its 1066 appearance (*circled above*). In the 17th century, the astronomer Edmond Halley noticed similarities between a comet he had seen in 1607 and one witnessed in 1682. He worked out that it was actually the same comet that passes Earth every 76 years. The last sighting of Halley's comet was in 1986.

After the Solar System was created about 4,500 million years ago, a lot of debris was left behind. The heavily-cratered faces of the inner four planets and the moons of the giants bear witness to a violent period of 'mopping up', when leftovers fell into the gravitational clutches of the planets and their moons. But the space between the planets and beyond is still full of a wide variety of small fry in the shape of comets, asteroids and dust.

Astronomers are particularly interested in these objects since they provide vital clues to unravelling the mystery of the origin of the Earth and other planets.

SPACE ALERT

It is now widely accepted that the extinction of the dinosaurs 60 million years ago was caused by the collision of a large meteorite with the Earth. Films such as *Deep Impact* (*above*) reflect the catastrophe that might happen if our planet were ever to be struck again. The possible threat from comets and meteorites is taken seriously by astronomers and governments alike. The sky is now being monitored for so-called Near-Earth Objects to provide warnings of possible future threats to Earth. Governments could then fire nuclear missiles into space to shatter the threat before it entered our atmosphere. However, if a really large meteorite were to head our way, we would simply stand no chance at all.

The Sun

Neptune's orbit

ASTEROIDS & METEORITES

Asteroids are rocks left over from when the planets were formed. They are found mainly between the orbits of Mars and Jupiter. Meteorites are chunks of stone that have broken off from asteroids and fall from space to Earth. Sometimes they are big enough to leave large craters, like the Barringer Crater in Arizona (left), which measures over 1 km (0.6 miles) across. It was created 50,000 years ago by the impact of a 50-metre-wide meteorite. The explosion was equivalent to 20 megatonnes of TNT detonating.

COSMIC CATASTROPHES

Cosmic catastrophes are not limited to the Earth. In July 1994, Comet Shoemaker-Levy 9 split into numerous fragments that collided with Jupiter. The dark stains on these four images of Jupiter are the impact sites. An event such as this on Earth would be devastating.

SCIENCE EXPLAINED: THE OORT CLOUD

In 1952 the Dutch astronomer Jan Oort suggested that comets come from a giant cloud surrounding the Sun, extending out to a distance of two light years beyond our Solar System. Oort suggested that occasionally gravitational disturbances caused by passing stars would nudge comets in towards the Sun. As they get closer, they develop the familiar gas and dust tails.

COMETS

Comets are chunks of ice mixed with dust — material left behind when the Sun and planets formed. Because of this, they are often described as 'dirty snowballs'. They either follow elliptical orbits around the Sun or get thrown out of the Solar System altogether. Some comets like Halley's Comet, have elongated orbits (*left*), which means they take a long time to go around the Sun.

As a comet plunges towards the Sun, its icy nucleus gives off gas, forming a bright glowing centre called a coma. When the comet reaches the inner part of the Solar System, a gas tail forms. The pressure of sunlight pushes away the loosened dust to form a curved dust tail. Occasionally, comets leave debris called meteors as they orbit the Sun. When they enter the Earth's atmosphere and burn up in the night sky, we refer to them as 'shooting stars'.

Gas tail

Dust tail

Coma

Pluto's orbit

HYDROGEN INTO HELIUM

The incredible amount of energy needed by the Sun is produced by a complex process in which hydrogen is converted into helium (*see also page 8*). This can be explained by Einstein's theory that a small mass loss creates vast amounts of energy. In the case of the Sun, this process gives off such a colossal amount of energy that the Sun is able to burn at a temperature of 15 million degrees at its core.

PROTON

NEUTRON

1. Two hydrogen protons join together to form a hydrogen proton-neutron pair called deuterium. Two protons are left over to repeat the entire process.

HELIUM^3

2. This pair is then joined by another hydrogen proton to make the nucleus of a helium^3 atom.

3. Next, two helium^3 nuclei join together to produce one stable helium atom (like the helium used to heat hot-air balloons).

STABLE HELIUM

PROTON

4. Because the mass of the four protons in the stable helium atom is too high, two protons disappear, creating energy. The spare protons then take part in future reactions.

SCIENCE EXPLAINED: THE SUN'S HEARTBEAT

Using a technique called spectroscopy, astronomers can measure how the surface of the Sun regularly approaches and recedes from the Earth over a period of five minutes. This pulsating causes the surface to vibrate like a drum. These 'drumbeats' are then analysed mathematically to reveal details of the structure of the Sun that had previously been unknown.

THE SUN

The Sun is a star that gives heat and light to the Solar System. It is a huge fiery gas ball over 300,000 times the size of the Earth. By converting hydrogen to helium, it makes vast amounts of energy. This hydrogen burning is the same reaction that occurs in hydrogen bombs. Without this energy, there would be no life on Earth. The Sun burns 400 tonnes of hydrogen in a second, but thankfully there is enough left to last another 5,000 million years!

Penumbra

Umbra

Photosphere

Chromosphere

Convective zone

Radiative zone

Core

SUNSPOTS

The Sun has an 11-year cycle of activity in which dark patches called sunspots (*above*) gradually start to appear on the surface. Sunspots can dwarf the Earth in size. They appear darker because they are 1,600 degrees cooler than the 6,000-degree photosphere. The dark centre of a sunspot is called the umbra and the region between the umbra and the photosphere is the penumbra.

ANGRY ERUPTIONS

Prominences are giant clouds that arch over the Sun and then fall back to its surface. They are far less energetic than flares and look dark when seen against the photosphere. This picture (*right*) shows a very active Sun with a vast prominence. The Earth would be a mere speck in comparison to this mighty eruption.

NEVER LOOK DIRECTLY AT THE SUN, EITHER WITH AN OPTICAL AID OR WITH THE NAKED EYE! IF YOU DO, YOU WILL RUN A SERIOUS RISK OF BEING BLINDED, AS MAY HAVE HAPPENED TO GALILEO. THE ONLY CORRECT WAY TO OBSERVE THE SUN IS TO PROJECT ITS IMAGE ON TO A PIECE OF PAPER OR CARD.

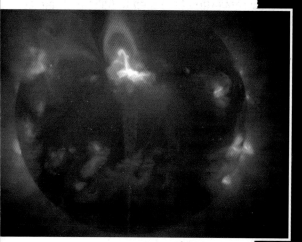

FLARES & SPACE WEATHER

A flare is an extremely energetic explosion that begins in the chromosphere and gets bigger when it reaches the corona. Flares emit very high energy X-rays and charged particles that reach Earth and occasionally wreak havoc with communications. This spectacular flare (*above*) is seen ripping its way through the corona. Flares are so dangerous that the Sun's activity is monitored daily by the Space Environment Center in the United States.

STRUCTURE OF THE SUN

Sunlight has a hard time reaching us. After it is forged in the core of the Sun, it gets bounced about for a million years in what is called the radiative zone. Even then its troubles aren't over. It now has to penetrate the bubbling convective zone before finally reaching the photosphere, which is the part of the Sun's surface that we see. Above the photosphere, there is the thick lower atmosphere called the chromosphere. Above that, and stretching beyond the Earth, is the thin corona, the visible part of which we see during an eclipse.

Photosphere

THE MILKY WAY & OTHER GALAXIES

THE MILKY WAY

The Milky Way has fascinated mankind for thousands of years, but it was Galileo (*above*) who first observed it through a telescope and found that it was made of **millions of stars.** Parts of the Milky Way can easily be seen in the night sky (*see pages 6-7*). Through a pair of binoculars you can see that it is actually made up of clusters of faint stars. We can only see a bit of the Milky Way, however, because most of our galaxy is blotted out by dust. Astronomers use radio waves to 'see' the whole picture.

It was only in the 20th century that we discovered that we live in a galaxy that is merely one among countless others. Galaxies are vast star systems and are the largest individual bodies in the Universe. There are many different types of galaxy, from dwarf types to giant galaxies that show violent activity at their centres, where they harbour massive black holes (*see page 24*).

SCIENCE EXPLAINED:
MAPPING OUR GALAXY WITH RADIO WAVES

Radio waves are so long that they can penetrate the clouds of dust that hide most of our galaxy from view. Free hydrogen atoms in space emit radio waves at a wavelength of 21 cm (8 inches). If the atom emitting the radio waves is moving away from us, this will cause the wavelength to appear slightly longer. If the source is approaching us the wavelength will be shorter. This enables radio astronomers to map galaxies. The technique has been used to reveal the long spiral arms of the Milky Way stretching outwards to the edge of the disc.

QUASARS

These astronauts are holding a model of the Chandra X-Ray Observatory, which is expected to allow researchers to obtain much better X-ray images of quasars. Quasars are a mystery. They are so far away from us that they look like very faint stars. In reality, they are blazing beacons as bright as an entire galaxy and are located in the most distant reaches of the Universe.

Elliptical

Spiral

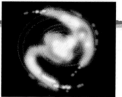
Barred Spiral

Irregular

THE GALAXY ZOO

Edwin Hubble classified galaxies into elliptical, spiral, barred and irregular types. Almost three-quarters of the galaxies in the Universe are elliptical — shaped like eggs. Spiral galaxies have a familiar shape, with the arms emerging from the central bulge (the Milky Way is a spiral galaxy). Barred galaxies are similiar in shape but have a central bridge of stars linking the inner ends of the spiral arms. Finally, irregular galaxies are galaxies that do not fit into any of these shapes.

THE MILKY WAY: AN ARTIST'S IMPRESSION

Because of the large amount of dust from inside the disc region, we cannot see very deeply into the Milky Way without the use of infrared and radio-wave technology.

This illustration shows what our galaxy probably looks like when seen from above. The central bulge contains stars but almost no gas or dust, while the disc region contains spiral arms that contain gas, dust and young stars. Our Solar System is located somewhere in the Orion arm.

Bulge

Disc region

Orion arm

STELLAR POPULATIONS

During the Second World War the German astronomer Walter Baade discovered that stars are distributed in galaxies according to age. In spiral galaxies such as ours, young stars (together with the giant clouds from which they were born) appear in the disc region, whereas the bulge is full of old stars. In elliptical galaxies all the stars are old. Baade laid the foundations for all future work on the life histories of stars and galaxies with his findings. In the galaxy NGC 2997 (*right*), we see the young (blue) stars of the disc region and the old (yellow) stars of the bulge.

Bulge   Disc region

DEADLY HOLES

Sometimes a supernova explosion leaves behind a remnant that is too massive even for a neutron star. When this happens, the star disappears altogether and becomes a black hole. The nucleus gets crushed into such a tiny volume that the extreme gravitational pull of the core closes up the space around it, preventing even light from escaping. Black holes cannot be seen, but their presence can be detected because they swallow surrounding matter. The matter spirals into the black hole and forms a disc that gets so hot that it emits X-rays. These can be detected by space probes. As you approach a black hole you start to feel its gravitational pull get stronger. The closer you get, the more speed you will need to escape its tight clutches. If you were foolhardy enough to enter the barrier of blackness known as the 'event horizon', you would never get out again. If you were really reckless and ventured anywhere near the centre, you would be sucked out of existence!

Outer region

Middle region

Inner region

SCIENCE EXPLAINED: SPACE-TIME

At the beginning of the last century, Albert Einstein invented a theory in which space and time joined together to form space-time. His theory explains many things that ordinary physics leaves unexplained, such as the famous twin paradox. This states that if one of two twins leaves the Earth and travels close to the speed of light, when he returns, he will be younger than his twin! Despite sounding incredible, it should be said that many of Einstein's predictions have been found to be correct.

Electrons

Atomic nuclei

NEUTRON STARS

Neutron stars are are born when gravity forces a star to collapse to such an extent that its electrons are forced together inside the atomic nuclei (*see above*). The resulting neutron star can be as small as 30 km (19 miles) across. They have intense magnetic fields and spin very quickly, some at over a hundred times per second.

Neutron stars are also intensely magnetic. These two factors cause them to emit their light in the form of two beams on opposite sides of the star (*right*). Neutron stars whose beams we can see are called pulsars.

COSMIC PUZZLERS

When stars like the Sun die, they end their days as **white dwarfs.** Stars that start out ten times bigger than the Sun, however, face a very different fate. The remnants left by such explosions are far denser than white dwarfs and can become either small superdense objects called neutron stars or black holes. Black holes suck matter out of the Universe, like vast whirlpools. Even stranger are wormholes. They are thought to link parts of the Universe by time tunnels that might conceivably make time travel possible.

EXPLOSION!

Supergiant stars rush through their fuel supply and die in a cataclysmic explosion that outshines a billion Suns. Two things happen during a supernova explosion. First, the outer shell of gas is blasted away, as shown in this picture of the Crab Nebula. There is also an inward implosion, which compresses the star's core to even higher densities than those of white dwarfs. At this point the core will become either a neutron star or a black hole.

TIME TRAVELLER

Many science fiction films explore the possiblity of time travel. In *The Terminator*, a deadly robot is sent back in time by an evil dictatorship to try to kill a woman who will give birth to the leader of a rebel army. Although this is science fantasy, some astronomers believe that time travel might theoretically be possible because of the existence of space phenomena called wormholes. These are supposed to connect distant parts of the Universe by a kind of tunnel in space-time. Just like in a black hole, time slows to a standstill, and the known laws of the Universe stop working. If a wormhole could be kept open long enough, it might be possible to travel through unharmed.

WHERE DID IT ALL BEGIN?

Some astronomers, such as Sir Fred Hoyle (*far right*), do not believe that life would have had sufficient time to develop to its present level of complexity in the 4,500 million years that the Earth has existed. They argue that the chances of DNA-type molecules evolving from simple carbon molecules are far too slim, and that this could only have happened long before the Earth was created. If the Universe is 15,000 million years old, as claimed by the Big Bang Theory (*see pages 28–29*), astronomers believe that there would have been enough time for DNA to evolve in space. Life molecules would then have been delivered to the Earth by close approaching comets. This idea is called the Panspermia Theory.

LIFE NOT AS WE KNOW IT

Science fiction writers have invented all sorts of strange beings to populate the Universe, such as E.T. (*right*), the extraterrestrial from the Steven Spielberg blockbuster. All known forms of life are based on the carbon atom, so astronomers look for traces of carbon-based molecules elsewhere in the Galaxy. Both have been found in comets, meteorites and the clouds from which stars form. The existence of life elsewhere is still fiercely debated, but the chances of finding it are looking good.

LOOKING FOR E.T.

Is there other intelligent life in the Universe? Have we been visited by extraterrestrials? Some have claimed that spacemen built the Egyptian pyramids, while supposed flying saucer sightings are regularly reported. An astronomer's answer to all this is to point out that, as far as we know, nothing can travel faster than light and that the distances between stars are simply too great for such travel to be possible. The existence of extraterrestrials is not questioned, just their ability to travel such huge distances in a reasonable time.

AN INTELLIGENT UNIVERSE

An idea that has received a lot of attention from astronomers over recent years is that the Universe is built in such a way that it demands the existence of human life. This is called the Anthropic Principle. Going even further, the British astronomer Sir Fred Hoyle (*above*) has suggested that human intelligence is part of a chain of intelligences with the Universe itself at the top of the chain.

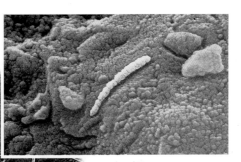

IS ANYBODY THERE?

The discovery of a simple single-celled organism embedded in a meteorite from Mars (*above*) was greeted with wild enthusiasm by astronomers, but most of us are really interested in knowing whether there are other intelligent beings in space. A project called SETI (Search for Extraterrestrial Intelligence) has been set up. This searches the sky with the largest radio telescope in the world at Arecibo in Puerto Rico (*left*). The amount of data obtained is so huge that the SETI programme has invited all owners of computers to download SETI software to help look for signals from extraterrestrials.

SCIENCE EXPLAINED: TRAVELLING TO THE STARS

To give an idea of how difficult travel between the stars is, imagine that we could make our spaceships travel at 1,100 km (660 miles) per second, a hundred times faster than the speed needed to escape the Earth's pull. Even at such a speed it would still take 1,000 years to reach the nearest star, just a few light years away! Our Galaxy is 100,000 light years wide, and our spaceship would take 25 million years to cross it. So unless extraterrestrials have far more advanced technology than we do, they are not likely to reach us in the foreseeable future.

HOW WILL IT ALL END?

What will be the eventual fate of the Universe? Everything depends on how dense the Universe is. There are three possibilities. If the density is higher than a certain value (the 'critical density'), then the Universe will eventually stop expanding and collapse in on itself. This is called the Big Crunch Scenario. If the density is less than critical, then the Universe will just go on expanding, and the temperature of everything in the Universe will plummet. Everything will become freezing cold. This scenario is called the Heat Death Scenario. Finally, if the density is just borderline, the Universe will expand less and less but will not collapse. This is called the Flat Universe Scenario. Boomerang (*left*), a balloon experiment sent high into the atmosphere above the Antarctic, measured the 'bumpiness' in the cosmic background. This measurement shows that the Universe is actually flat. In other words, neither the Big Crunch nor the Heat Death scenario will happen.

SCIENCE EXPLAINED: HUBBLE'S LAW

Edwin Hubble was the first to suggest that the galaxies are moving away from us. This idea was later developed into the theory of the expanding Universe. Hubble also discovered that the speed with which a galaxy moves away from us depends on its distance. The farther away from us a galaxy is, the faster it moves. This important law can be used to find the distance of a remote galaxy from the speed of recession.

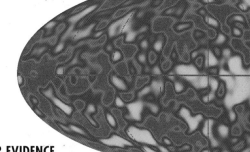

OTHER EVIDENCE

Apart from the expansion of the Universe, there are other important pieces of evidence in favour of the Big Bang theory. After any explosion, a fireball expands and cools. In the case of the Big Bang, the original fireball occurred about 15 billion years ago and should by now have a temperature of 270 degrees below zero. The image of the Universe taken by the COBE satellite (*above right*) confirmed this temperature.

EXPANSION OF THE UNIVERSE

The galaxies all appear to be shooting away from us at very great speeds. This is not because we occupy any special position in the Universe — exactly the same thing would be observed from any other galaxy. In fact, it is not the galaxies that are moving, but the space between them that is expanding. Imagine sticking stars on a balloon and then blowing the balloon up. The stars would seem to move apart as the balloon inflates. The expansion of the Universe is a process that has been occurring over billions of years.

THE BIG BANG & THE FATE OF THE UNIVERSE

One of the key questions that cosmologists are always trying to solve is how the Universe was created. They believe that the Universe came into being about 15 billion years ago in a huge explosion called the Big Bang. From being squashed together in a tight ball, matter suddenly expanded outwards, eventually creating the stars and planets. Astronomers are also trying to work out how the Universe will end, and have come up with a number of different scenarios.

THE BEGINNING OF EVERYTHING

If the Universe is expanding, could this mean that the galaxies started out from a dense clump of matter at some time in the past? Imagine filming the explosion of a shell in the air. After the explosion, we see fragments of shell rushing away from one another. If we rewind the film, we will come to the original unexploded shell. Most astronomers now believe that the expansion of the Universe started from the explosion of a fireball some 15 billion years ago. This explosion is known as the Big Bang.

CREATING CONDITIONS FOR LIFE

Today, conditions on Earth are perfect for life, allowing a huge diversity of creatures to flourish. However, these conditions have taken billions of years to evolve. Astronomers believe the Universe has gone through several stages since the Big Bang. During the initial fireball the temperature was a staggering 10 billion degrees. After 30,000 years the temperature dropped to 10,000 degrees, still far too hot for life to stand a chance. During this period, called the 'radiation era', matter and radiation formed an impenetrable soup. After the radiation era came the 'matter era', when matter became separated from the radiation. The Universe became transparent and its temperature dropped to the present chilly 270 degrees below zero.

ASTRONOMY TODAY & IN THE FUTURE

If astronomy today looks exciting, astronomy in the future will be truly mouthwatering! Major advances are being made on a regular basis. New giant telescopes are being built to help astronomers peer farther into space, while new sites for telescopes are being planned in the Antarctic to take advantage of the excellent conditions there. The future also looks likely to bring an observatory on the Moon and possibly even Mars, but this is only the beginning for the astronomy of tomorrow. There is even talk of sending a space submarine to Jupiter's moon Europa to probe for life in its frozen oceans.

HOLIDAYS IN SPACE

Civilians have been going into space for some years now, but Dennis Tito's trip in 2001 was very different. Tito paid his own tourist-class fare – some 20 million dollars! There is now an International Space Station in Earth orbit, but its living quarters are (so far) for working astronauts, and were not intended as a hotel for tourists. Now a long line of millionaires are queuing up for a once-in-a-lifetime space jaunt. It is likely that before the century is out, ordinary people will be able to fly to the Moon, Mars and maybe beyond.

A SUBMARINE TO EUROPA?

Europa is a hostile moon bathed in dangerous radiation from Jupiter. Nevertheless, astronomers are keen to go there because they think that there are oceans beneath its frozen surface. Some kind of robotic submarine probe could be sent from Earth to explore the Europan oceans for possible life. These oceans would be in permanent darkness because of the thickness of the overlaying ice, but then so are the bottoms of the Earth's oceans, and yet there is life there – two-metre-long worms have been found near volcanic vents on the ocean beds.

GREAT ARRAY

The power of a telescope to display fine detail is decided by the width of its primary mirror. If two telescopes are used together they only collect as much light as the combined size of the two mirrors will permit. However, their combined power to display fine detail is determined by the distance separating them. Large arrays of optical and radio telescopes have already been built, and there are ambitious plans to build even more powerful ones in the future. Besides the high mountain sites in La Palma and Hawaii, astronomers have also begun to base installations in the Antarctic. With its very dry air, providing excellent conditions for infrared work, Antarctica looks set to become increasingly important in the future of astronomy.

A LUNAR OBSERVATORY?

With a permanent manned base on the Moon, astronomers will almost certainly put large telescopes there. The main benefit to astronomers from permanent space observatories will be access at all times to all parts of the spectrum, especially the infrared, ultraviolet, X-ray and gamma ray regions (*see pages 4-5*). For the more immediate future, there are several large space projects being planned, such as the Next Generation Space Telescope. This will collect almost four times more light than the Hubble Space Telescope.

GLOSSARY

Asteroid – Lumps of rock left over when the planets in the Solar System were formed, mostly found in a zone called the asteroid belt between Mars and Jupiter.

Atom – The smallest chemical unit of matter, made up of a nucleus surrounded by orbiting electrons.

Black hole – Superdense object with such a high concentration of matter and gravity that not even light can escape.

Comet – A chunk of ice and dust that orbits the Sun.

Constellation – A grouping of stars in the sky, named after characters in Greek and Roman mythology.

Density – The amount of mass divided by the amount of space a planet occupies.

Dwarf – The name given to a newly formed star when it begins to convert its hydrogen into helium.

Einstein's theory of relativity – Theory of gravity devised by Albert Einstein (1879–1955) that applies to massive objects with intense gravitational fields.

Electron – A negatively charged particle that orbits a nucleus.

Galaxy – A gigantic gathering of stars, the biggest single unit in the Universe.

Galaxy cluster – A collection of galaxies. A really large grouping is called a supercluster.

Giant – A swollen star that has left the main sequence.

Globular cluster – A grouping of up to 100,000 old stars tightly bound together by gravity.

Luminosity – The amount of radiation given off at the surface of a star or planet.

Meteor – Debris left behind by comets, visible as a luminous vapour trail when it enters the Earth's atmosphere.

Meteorite – A chunk of rock that has broken off from asteroids and plummeted to Earth.

Molecule – A clump of two or more atoms.

Neutron – A neutral particle forming part of the atomic nucleus.

Neutron star – A heavily compressed star left over from the explosion of a supernova.

Newton's theory of gravity – Theory devised by Sir Isaac Newton (1642-1727) stating that all objects are attracted to each other. The more massive the objects, the stronger the attraction, but this attraction diminishes as objects get more distant from one another.

Open cluster – A large family of up to 10,000 young stars in the plane of the Milky Way.

Proton – A positively charged particle forming part of the atomic nucleus.

Spectrum – The light from a star or galaxy split up into wavelengths of different colours.

Supergiant – A former hot, bright main sequence star that has swollen to many times its original size.

White dwarf – A dead star left behind in the centre of a planetary nebula.

ACKNOWLEDGEMENTS

We would like to thank Advocate and Elizabeth Wiggans for their assistance.
Illustrations by John Alston, Simon Mendez, Peter Bull and Paul Davies.
Copyright © 2001 ticktock Publishing Ltd.
First published in Great Britain by ticktock Publishing Ltd., Century Place, Lamberts Road, Tunbridge Wells, Kent TN2 3EH, U.K. All rights reserved.
No part of this publication may be reproduced, stored in a retrieval system, or transmitted in any form or by any means electronic, mechanical, photocopying, recording or otherwise, without prior written permission of the copyright owner.
A CIP catalogue record for this book is available from the British Library. ISBN 1 86007 258 5 (paperback). ISBN 1 86007 262 3 (hardback). 1 2 3 4 5 6 7 8 9 10.
Printed in Malta

t=top, b=bottom, c=centre, l=left, r=right, OFC=outside front cover, IFC=inside front cover, IBC=inside back cover, OBC=outside back cover

Art Archive: 3br, 18tl, 22tl. Corbis Images: 16b, 19t, 27tr, 27t, 29b, 31t. Kobal Collection: 14c, 25b, 19b, 26b. NASA: 2tl, 3tr, 8cr, 9cl, 9b, 12cl, 12b, 13tr, 14tl, 15tl, 15cr, 15cl, 15c, 16tl, 16tr, 16-17c, 16br, 16tr, 17tr, 17br, 19cl, 20tl, 21tl, 23tr, 25tr. National Maritime Museum: 2bl. Popperfoto: 22b, 30tl. Science Photo Library: OBC, 21r, 26b, 26cl, 31b. Tony Stone: 12-13c.

Every effort has been made to trace the copyright holders and we apologize in advance for any unintentional omissions. We would be pleased to insert the appropriate acknowledgement in any subsequent edition of this publication.

snapping-turtle guide